50 COFFEES

JENNY MOATES

DEDICATION

At the heart of what has shaped this book are some special people in my community. First, I am grateful to my "founding 50 coffees" who, without you, this book would not have been possible. Specifically to Coffee #23, thank you for reminding me why I was writing this book when I doubted my purpose. To my business partner and lifelong friend, Yvette, your unfailing loyalty and love for more than 30 years is a priceless treasure. For my children Rylie, Lily and Brody, I pray that you will believe in your dreams and know that, with God, all things are possible. And to Brian, I cannot adequately find the words for how you have influenced my life as both my husband and best friend. You've always seen more in me than I've seen in myself. I love you.

Anything good that you see in me is because of my Lord and Savior, Jesus Christ.

CONTENTS

INTRODUCTION

January 10, 2012 ~ I came out of my "survival bubble" as I sat quietly thinking about the new year ahead. It was my daughter's 3rd birthday, my son was now 18-months old and my oldest daughter 7. After what seemed like a lifetime of surviving the responsibilities as a mom and business owner, I was thoroughly exhausted. Happy...but exhausted. I had lost sight of everything else in the world, including my work. But now, my three little humans had gained more independence and I could focus on other things.

I began to have a fresh perspective about the company I founded, Moving Ideas, and viewed my leadership in a whole new light. We hadn't significantly grown in several years and had no strategy in place to get there. In the same breath, I felt an uneasy conviction about my ability to kickstart that change. This turning of the tide has led to one of the biggest transformations in my life.

Until this point, I had spent the better part of my career as a designer and producer in marketing communications. Every day I poured energy into creating one new project after another – getting pretty good at "what I do." And, as any entrepreneur hopes for, our firm had become highly respected by colleagues and clients. But as I mentioned, our client base had not grown or diversified in years. Our revenue was stagnant and unstable. We didn't know what to expect or count on from one month to the next.

When I asked myself 'How did this happen?' I discovered that being good at "what I do" had put me in a professional vacuum. Focusing on the work alone had sucked me into a space that left very little oxygen for my company to grow. It had isolated me from any efforts to meet others outside of my microcosm and family life. Not only did my business need attention, but my business partner and the team of people around us deserved better leadership from me.

As I looked (with honesty) at some hard questions, "What impact are you making on others? Your work? The future of your company?" I started to understand something much bigger. I could feel it poking on my subconscious and I would not be satisfied until I figured it out.

This book is about how I forced myself to get out of a self-imposed bubble and connect with others to grow my "community." I did this through – you guessed it – having 50 coffee meetings with strangers over the better part of a year. But it ended up going far beyond cappuccinos and conversations. With each diverse encounter, I learned to be more myself and more eager to learn about others, rather than learning what others could do for me.

My mindset and ultimately the course of my life has been changed because of my 50 coffees. I hope my journey will inspire you to intentionally broaden your horizons, whether it's over coffee, lunch or another activity of your choice. Because what I discovered was the true power in relationships, an art that tends to be overlooked in our "Just send me an email" and "No thanks, I'm not interested in what you are selling" culture.

Each chapter is punctuated with an "espresso shot" – an ounce of tribal wisdom from what I've learned. After reading, I also hope you will join me in our 50 Coffees group on Facebook... where we're always open and the coffee and conversations are flowing.

"INNOVATING YOURSELF IS A LIFELONG PURSUIT."

AN ISLAND OF MYSELF

———~~~———

"YOU CAN'T CREATE ANYTHING MEANINGFUL ON AN ISLAND. IT TAKES A COMMUNITY OF PEOPLE... AND LOTS OF GOOD COFFEE."

Within a five-hour drive, there's a ferry to one of my favorite destinations on the planet, *Bald Head Island*. And, for 364 days each year, I look forward to that happy moment when my family, closest friends and our two dogs will climb onto that floating transport taking us away from work, schedules and life's stresses back on shore. Pulling away from the dock I can physically feel my blood pressure lowering.

In the days that follow, we spend our treasured

time sipping coffee at sunrise, playing in the sand and logging precious memories into our book of life. My soul will literally be reset back to its natural, God-given position of harmony. But, when it's time to pack up and go home again, I can't help but want just one more week or at the least, one more sunset.

The allure and peace of an island is captivating to many of us but there is a flip side to this curious geography. These small sections of earth are only attached to the sea floor. They are completely surrounded by water with no natural land bridge attaching them to a continent. Islands offer no immediate access to the mainland, so you must rely solely on what you have readily available to meet your needs. Thankfully, BHI has a small grocery store, a few good restaurants and an icecream shop – all the essentials of a well-planned vacation. But, if you're like me and you have a tendency to overthink things, islands are only appealing to us under those ideal circumstances like vacations and getaways.

I'm not sure which summer it was, but we felt a small sampling of what it would be like to live on the island that year. My family and I are avid movie lovers and we dedicate most of our Friday evenings to "family movie night." Days before the trip, we learned that the latest Harry Potter movie would be released in theaters. We were all anxious to see it and pretty bummed we'd have to wait the extra week to watch it back on the mainland. I actually entertained the idea of ferrying everyone to and from Southport, the small coastal city closest to us. But considering the outrageous cost, we opted to wait. My point is, given the smallest inconvenience or possibly something much bigger – like the threat of a hurricane or injury – over time my beloved vacation spot might feel more like isolation.

Business isolation is no different. In my pre-50 Coffees mindset, I was 100% guilty of building tall borders around my daily work life. I was the queen of busy and couldn't see past my own work nose to realize how much I was missing. Specifically, I began to realize my shortcomings in this area when I was invited to lunch by a colleague. Lunch was obviously not out of the ordinary but this particular lunch would require me to spend time getting to know two new business contacts. It sounds harmless enough but my honest first reaction was, "I don't feel up to meeting new people today." The idea of taking time out of my busy day for a longer-than-usual lunch with people I had never met before just didn't sound appealing to me. My colleague looked at me in horror when I responded with that honest, "Today?" reaction. He had clearly been able to see the bigger picture and had the foresight to know that our lunch dates could be potential new clients, or at the very least, respectable human beings who have value to add in this world. And he was right on both accounts. I begrudgingly tagged along and began what has become a long-term business relationship with one gentleman from that lunch. He is a fantastic human being and has time-and-time-again been an advocate for my business. We've partnered on several important brand initiatives together and I'm embarrassed to admit that they have been financially fruitful as well.

Now that my own viewpoint has shifted, I'm able to see the same shortsightedness in others who are missing out on genuine opportunities. Just the other day I made an introduction to two colleagues which, in my opinion, would have been truly beneficial for both of them. One who I will call "tech startup guy" is in the entrepreneurial stages of a new technology solution that directly touches the retail consumer market. The other, a "retail brand expert," has a stout background in delivering marketing experiences for national retail brands. This made perfect sense to me, so I did what comes naturally to me now and introduced the two of them. But what happened next surprised me. Tech startup guy (who I really like and admire) misperceived the introduction as a solicitation for new business. In fairness to him, I may have worded my email wrong but this was not a networking attempt to feed business to my retail brand expert.

This story ends like a dud firework that never goes off. No meeting or continued exploration, just a "thanks for the introduction but we don't have a need for that type of thing right now." Being copied on this email I was shaking my head thinking, 'Wow! That was the old me before 50 Coffees.'

We may never know what insight or value each could have brought into that relationship and moreover, how that could have impacted both of them professionally or otherwise. To put it another way, for just one hour of time over coffee, tech-startup-guy could have expanded his community reach. It may not have impacted him today, but somewhere down the road, having retail-brand-expert's insight could have been beneficial. Or maybe (and the 'what ifs' go on and on) retail-brand-expert would have a conversation with one of his former clients (national retail brand execs) and think about tech-startup-guy's solution, making another introduction. I'm sure that both of my colleagues will be perfectly fine moving forward but my point is that *collaboration is better*.

Albert Einstein, the brilliant Nobel Prize recipient and theoretical physicist, knew the importance of community and collaboration with others. While many of us may imagine him to have been a lone genius, he was known to collaborate with recognized and various other scientists on numerous experiments. His own namesake institution "Albert Einstein College of Medicine" has a "Collaboration Zone" for clinicians, clinical investigators and researchers who wish to collaborate on new disease research. Perhaps his genius and his greatest legacy is that he recognized the tremendous benefits in working together to achieve great things.

Looking closely at the reason why tech-startup-guy and retail-brand-expert could not find a connection, I've concluded two things. One, we have a natural tendency, perhaps for many cultural reasons, to perceive business interactions as a "what's in it for me?" frame of mind. And, two, we minimize the impact that collaborating with others could make on us – both individually and for our businesses.

So how do we start collaborating and stop focusing on our own self interests? How do we get off of that island of ourselves? We can start by building land bridges (relationships) that have the potential to eventually grow our community and ultimately expand our reach. And, the lifelong effects of that reach are limitless.

RELATIONSHIPS BUILD COMMUNITY.
COMMUNITY INCREASES REACH.
REACH AFFECTS RETURN.

CAFFEINATED AWAKENING

In January 2012, half asleep and sipping coffee from our kitchen table, I turned to my highly sociable husband and said, "How do you know so many people?" Oddly, my question felt as juvenile as the boy eating Cheerios on my lap and that's when it hit me... I was stuck in the infant stages of building my business community and had very few relationships to show for the years I had lived and worked in Charlotte.

"You should have coffee with people," he answered. This was easy for the person who lived on caffeine and could navigate any coffee house from here to South Carolina. But beyond that, he was a recruiter. It was his job to meet people. In fact, his job *required* a certain number of new connections each week.

But meeting up with unfamiliar people seemed strange and was honestly not a comfortable idea to wrap my head around. Having owned Moving Ideas, a small brand communications firm, for eight years, I had fallen into a trap I believe many business owners and professionals can relate to. It's what I call my "bubble of expertise." I had become uniquely good at "what I do" but not an expert at growing my business or strengthening my professional community.

As my husband and I talked more that morning, the reality of another new year began to sink in for both of us. We were in awe of how quickly the past few years had gone, nurturing newborns and building careers. But, it was time for something new.

You know that feeling you get when something is poking your subconscious and it can't be satisfied until you have figure it out? That was *this*. This overwhelming sensation, or as I like to call it 'my caffeinated awakening,' began to happen. My mind was feeling a jolt of dark roast perspective.

I had lived on the island of myself and in my bubble for so long that I became numb to all of the potential that our firm was missing out on. I'm a successful brander and communicator but that's the only bubble that was safe and completely familiar.

And by now, you've figured out that I like my bubbles.

The problem was that my comfort impacted everything, including revenue. We were doing fine but certainly not thriving. Our firm managed to hang on but it was challenging to make a profit after the 2008 drop in the market.

Our clients appreciated the value we brought to their organizations and would occasionally give us a generous referral. But to be honest, bringing in new accounts was not something I or my business partner prioritized. If I had to rate this skill on a scale of 1-10, we probably ranked somewhere around two.

Don't get me wrong, we did meaningful work at an exceptional standard that kept our clients impressed. Typically, we experienced a steady flow of projects but there was very little in the way of NEW strategy and creative. On the rare occasion, when we had the opportunity to work with a new client on something different, the firm would buzz with excitement. Everyone on our team was reenergized. My senior designer and I could endlessly chat about ideas for the new project and strategists were digging deep into research to learn as much as they could about the new product or industry.

It wasn't obvious to me at the time but these new opportunities made our livelihood more lively again.

I learned first hand that business stagnation is dull and, by definition, fails to advance. Without *new opportunities* to work with *new clients* on *new initiatives*, we were limiting our economic, professional and personal growth.

In all of these areas, we were handicapping ourselves. We spent the majority of our time on the "what we do" and not on the "who we include" or relationships we were cultivating. By not being in community with others, we were hindering our reach.

Ironically, reach is a marketing term that we talk about in our firm. It's important because without having an audience to reach, we have no reason to develop communications. Whether the audience is B to B or direct to consumers, you have to reach those who are willing to buy and choose your product or service. It's that simple.

This is not a new concept. It goes as far back as the 1890s in early barn advertising which was made popular by the Bloch Brothers Tobacco Company. You could read "Treat Yourself to the Best" on barns for Mailpouch Tobacco. Roadside travelers caught on to what they were doing, so much so that eventually some 20,000 barns in 22 states showcased the effectiveness of their brand awareness campaign.

The concept of having healthy "reach" begs many questions, 'How can you expect to sell your products and services if no one knows about them?' or... 'How can the best people come to work for you if they don't know about your culture or opportunities?' or... 'How can you solve business problems without other like-minded people to share them with?' And the list of questions goes on. The same is true for all businesses. Having a healthy reach helps you to grow your customers, resources, revenue and gain your full market potential.

REACH IS BOTH AN ACTION TAKEN
AND AN ASSET TO BE TREASURED.

STRATEGY OF 50

Within a couple of days of my caffeinated awakening, I started processing the odd idea of having coffee with strangers... STRANGERS! Aren't those the people that our parents warned us about and didn't they tell us to run if they didn't know the secret code word? This is the stream of consciousness I had about the whole situation. Wouldn't it be easier to just avoid uncomfortable situations all together?

I am a fairly shy person. To meet me you would never know that. Even today, my stomach gets butterflies at the thought of social situations with new people and unknown surroundings. When I was young, I was painfully shy and didn't have much confidence. My parents enrolled me into a private elementary school in first grade at the under-age of five – when most people were attending Kindergarten. Midway through my senior year of high school I turned 17, when most of my classmates were turning 18. This was social awkwardness at its finest. Academically I was smart enough to be there but emotionally I was always a step behind everyone else at every milestone... boyfriends, puberty and driving just to name a few of the highlights. But college rescued me from that extremely awkward time and I've never looked back.

Thankfully, I met some kindred spirits in my freshman year at Embry Riddle University who grabbed me by the neck and called me their own. Many weekends were spent at the Sigma Chi fraternity with special people who became my home and created a safe environment for me to be myself. I spent several years with that tribe and looking back now, I know that they were instrumental in helping me come out of my shell.

So, when I reluctantly gave into this new idea of having coffee with strangers, my first thought was to set a goal. When you're a creative type, like me, you see the world as fluid and ever changing including priorities and direction. While this drives some, more pragmatic people, crazy that's my reality. With that being said, if I don't set a goal and publicly share it with the people who will hold me accountable, it will NEVER happen. I'm sure it goes back to some

Freudian, psychological fear of being seen naked in public which motivates me to follow through.

To set my goal, I needed to develop a strategy that worked well within the construct of my current work/life balance. I typically manage my work and children's activities on a week to week basis. It's rationally as much bandwidth as I have without overloading other areas of my life.

Looking at this in terms of a weekly commitment and giving myself a reasonable time frame to accomplish something meaningful, I considered the whole year in front of me, 52 weeks. As long as I protected Christmas and Thanksgiving weeks, that would make 50 coffees, one new coffee per week. So there it was, 50! Done, ready to start scheduling.

WHY COFFEE?

I started drinking coffee when I was barely reciting my ABCs. My grandmother's fragile and fancy antique demitasse cup set was especially charming to me in their pretty pink and pastel colors. Just my size, I would fill the fairy-sized cup almost to the brim with milk, then add sugar and top it off with a dash of coffee. Perfection! This began my attraction to this sublime liquid.

Some of my fondest memories involve gathering

around the table, sipping coffee and telling fantastic stories. Always a good time and full of laughter and happiness. That's something to shoot for in any initiative.

Coffee allows us to carve out time in the day, in a place that is comfortable and encourages community with another human being. It's the reason you can find a coffee shop on just about any corner of the globe.

Unlike lunch, coffee lessens the chance for etiquette errors and embarrassment over of who will pay the bill or eating with your mouth full. Coffee, tea or whatever satisfaction in a cup makes you happy is logical, efficient and inexpensive.

50 MATTERS

There was something about the quantity of 50 that felt right for me. A very interesting thing happened around coffee #15. My goal that seemed – to me – to be inconsequential in the scheme of life and business, was starting to feel much more important. I started taking audio notes from each new coffee to capture what I had learned that day. It's scientifically proven that it takes approximately 21 days to form a habit and that doing something new, consistently, will bring about a lasting change. 50, as it turned out for me, was a good number for my new habit of community building.

The relevance of a number like 50 became well-founded to me while having coffee with #26 – a marketing executive based in NYC but working in Charlotte. To give you a little background, she had returned to the states from Europe where, for years prior, she was the marketing director for an international company whose brands included a major vodka and women's handbag line. When I explained my coffee idea to her, she related her story – a single, professional who had been apprehensively involved in online dating.

Drop-dead-gorgeous and with a brilliant mind, she shared tales of the wide range of men she encountered living in the city and how the experience changed the way she looked at people. Bravely venturing into the world of online dating she hoped to meet the perfect man for her – tall, dark, handsome, smart, motivated, successful, etc. This is a woman who could probably win the heart and mind of any man she met. Ironically, the more dates she went on, the more she learned about others and herself. As we finished our Thai chicken salads (yes, sometimes lunch fits your schedule better), she admitted that meeting so many different men in her quest to find Mr. Right allowed her to become a more open person. It significantly changed her view of what she was hoping to find in her future husband, the Mr. Right-for-her.

Spending time with so many souls does shape a person. There's a refinement that happens in your interpersonal skills, that without practice, you won't realize the benefits. Relationships become easier to foster as your perspective of people broadens. You'll never be the same again.

MAKE YOUR GOALS PUBLIC SO THAT YOU WILL BE HELD ACCOUNTABLE.

ANTI-NETWORKING

Networking stinks. Trying to build a meaningful connection at a networking event is like throwing a handful of seeds on the ground and expecting a fruitful garden to appear six weeks later. It's pretty unlikely. Sure, these events can help you make initial contacts but you'll never get to know someone authentically in a crowded room of people by shooting business cards from your hip like a machine gun. Telling your business story in a 10-second pitch just isn't the stuff that relationships are built on.

This is true for a couple of reasons. You cannot establish a real link with someone in an awkward, rapid-fire environment. And, nobody is 100% comfortable introducing themselves to a room of foreign faces and pitching their business information –

which by the way, they hold near and dear to their heart. Most people are anxious on some level in a social environment. In a study that ranked America's top phobias, "fear of people or social situations" was ranked sixth in the top ten, right behind the "fear of heights" and "fear of spiders."

While 50 Coffees is certainly about building a strong network of colleagues, it is very much an "anti-networking" approach. Instead, this experience has taught me to rethink my relationships in the context of community. The word "community" is derived from the Latin "communis" which means things held in common, a broad term for fellowship. Taking a more beneficial pathway to authentic community with others brings us together socially, mentally and sometimes economically. It is in communities that we are able to have a more connected experience with shared intents, beliefs, resources, preferences, needs, risks and a number of other conditions that identify who we are.

Words matter, so much so that in my field of communications we regularly study definitions and synonyms of words to truly understand the depth of their intended meaning and how they influence behavior.

"WORDS ARE ALSO ACTIONS, AND ACTIONS ARE A KIND OF WORDS."
RALPH WALDO EMERSON

Take for example these Webster's meanings to help us compare the action of networking vs. the community concept.

Network ~ to form business contacts through informal social meetings

Community ~ a social group of any size whose members reside in a specific locality and often have a common cultural and historical heritage

A network is the *tip* of the iceberg but a community is the vast underside of a much larger mass. And isn't the mass what we really care about in business anyway? No one is truly satisfied with just a small, irrelevant portion of anything.

Just the word pictures of "social group" and "have a common cultural and historical heritage" in the framework of business, present a much richer and deeper way to be in alliance with others.

Now let's examine the synonyms of these ideas.

Network ~ web, grid, net, organization, structure, system, chain, arrangement, complex, hookup, jungle, labyrinth, maze, wiring

Community ~ association, center, company, district, neighborhood, people, public, society, state, colony, commonality, commonwealth, locality, residents, territory, turf, body, neck of the woods, stomping ground

I'm convinced that most of us would prefer "commonality" over "arrangement" and a "neighborhood" over a "system." And yes, this is semantics. But it does illustrate the greater point, which is that we as, professionals, need to be in community far more than we need a network, web or maze of contacts that we hardly know. What we're all hoping for as an outcome is a "sense of community."

In my research, I found a psychological study around the benefits of community. According to the study, a sense of community is made up of four key elements.

1. *Membership:* Having a sense of belonging and identification with a person or group. Membership also includes established boundaries, emotional safety, a personal investment and a common symbol system.

2. *Influence:* Members believe that they can make an impact on its members, have an effect in the group and in some way are needed for the group's cohesion.

3. *Integration and fulfillment of needs:* Members feel rewarded, large or small, for their

participation and can fulfill their individual needs. Members feel a sense of community.

4. *Shared emotional connection:* According to the theory, this is the 'definitive element for true connection.' This element consists of and is based on a shared history or participation with others, however short or long that history may be.

I love the example this study uses to illustrate the dynamics between these four elements:

"Someone puts an announcement on the dormitory bulletin board about the formation of an intramural dormitory basketball team. People attend the organizational meeting as strangers out of their individual needs (integration and fulfillment of needs). The team is bound by place of residence (membership boundaries are set) and spends time together in practice. They play a game and win (successful shared event). While playing, members exert energy on behalf of the team (personal investment in the group). As the team continues to win, team members become recognized and congratulated (gaining honor and status for being members). Someone suggests that they all buy matching shirts and shoes (common symbols) and they do so (influence)."[1]

1. Primary theoretical foundation: McMillan and Chavis

NETWORKING EVENTS ARE ONLY AS FRUITFUL
AS THE RELATIONSHIPS FOSTERED
OUTSIDE OF THE EVENT ITSELF.

LIVING
COMMUNITIES

~~~

Growing up in Florida, I was naturally intrigued by coral reefs. Their intelligent design and integration with global life is more influential than any business initiative we could ever hope to be associated with. Coral reefs teem with living organisms, plants and sea creatures. They cover less than one percent of the ocean floor, but their impact is incredible. Reefs are the "rainforests of the oceans." Human life *literally* depends upon their survival.

But what I find most interesting is HOW they've survived for hundreds and thousands of years. Dependent on how they live together, a coral reef is a community of living organisms that act as a single organism. Billions of polyps join forces to do more good for our planet than you might imagine. They protect shorelines, provide food for coastal populations and they are also the source for medications including anti-cancer drugs. They're influence is tremendous and they set a good example for us to consider in our own professional survival. To be active in the Great Barrier Reef of our lives, it's critical that we also view our community as one living organism.

Evidence of this can be found in our own living reefs... our neighborhoods. We've all seen or been a part of the heart warming evidence of groups who valiantly work in concert with one another to rally around a cause. Without individuals and organizations coming together, the hungry would go without enough meals, research around cancer treatment would disappear and many problems we face collectively would go unaddressed. The impact is much too big to quantify.

Several years ago, my team and I had the rare honor of developing the 25th anniversary annual report for our regional Make-A-Wish® chapter. Over the course of several weeks in planning, concepting, writing, designing and research, we learned firsthand what it means to be part of something much bigger than our daily work life, something extraordinary. Make-A-Wish is a wonderful, nonprofit organization that faithfully makes dreams come true for children with life-threatening medical conditions. They are inspired daily by the belief that granting these wishes and experiences can be a game-changer for some of them.

Will Dicus, a fifteen-year-old boy, knew all about the power of community and loved his teammates. He was a star baseball player on his high school team and was battling Acute Myeloid Leukemia. Like any teenage boy, his wish was to have his 2003 Blazer "pimped." With the help of several local businesses, volunteers, his family and friends, Will received his newly decked out Blazer at his 16th birthday party. With amazing determination during the most difficult times of his treatment, Will never let his team down, supporting them in whatever way he could. When Will passed, his team was there for him. In honor of their cherished friend, Will's entire team sat together at his funeral wearing their baseball uniforms.

This story and so many others are a sobering reminder of what's important – whose lives we touch and how much we give to them. A dear friend of ours, and former Make-A-Wish employee, spent time with us sharing many tearful and hopeful wish stories. Hundreds of volunteers, wish granters, fundraisers, donors and staff at Make-A-Wish are the reason they are able to do what they do. And while some of these people are famous celebrities, most are unknown and ordinary individuals. They serve behind the scenes to do something remarkable, donating their hearts, time, money, resources, airline miles, gifts in kind, and whatever is needed to make it happen.

My business, Moving Ideas, is like many of yours. We need the same thoughtful Make-A-Wish approach to not only survive but to survive well. For years our business model has been designed as one big community. We intentionally set out to make a living by harnessing the numerous and many talents of strategists, writers, photographers, videographers and designers. These virtual teammates orbit around our firm as satellites and their specific, unique abilities allow us to execute world class communications in a highly specialized and lean model. We couldn't do it without them.

Our virtual team is a living community continuously in motion. But when our clients hire us to develop a new brand, campaign, video or other initiative, we stop what we're doing to pull the team together for strategic brainstorming sessions. And, depending on the project, we also invite guest experts with specific industry experience to lend a creative hand. Developing the right ideas and concepts is dependent upon this part of our process. For us, this is the fun stuff. So we eagerly gather around the whiteboard ready to contribute to the day's collective thinking. Everyone in the room makes an impact because we rely completely on their diverse thoughts, knowledge, wisdom and experiences. Our brightest, most successful creative concepts have come out of these sessions. They work because of three key factors:

1. We have an established relationship and are in community with one another.
2. Everyone gives something and contributes.
3. The ideas are expansive and have reach well beyond our own.

"WITH" IS A SMALL, YET INCREDIBLY SIGNIFICANT WORD.

THE REALLY REAL
HOUR

THE REAL YOU

Dr. Seuss says it best: "Today you are You, that is truer than true. There is no one alive who is Youer than You."

How many times have you gone into a new encounter with butterflies in your stomach and your best game face on? I'm not saying that it's wrong to be nervous or guarded because, after all, you are meeting someone for the first time. But what's *not* OK is to bring a not-so-real representation of yourself.

When we begin building relationships with someone new, the absolute worst thing to do is to be something you're not. Polished, buttoned up, careful, cool cat.. whatever it is that you assume people care about... you're probably wrong. Taking this approach will not make the other person comfortable or willing to open up to you. Only the power of the real you can do that. If not, your coffee appointment will merely grin and bare their way through the next hour and to make matters worse, they'll mirror your approach. The entire exchange will be an utter waste of everyone's time.

My mother has been preaching my entire life 'there is no one in the world like you. God made us all different for a reason.' So why do we instinctively default to our public persona and throw on these masks? We see this kind of behavior pronounced in celebrities today. They want so much to be seen as perfect and irresistible yet the tabloid pages are filled with candid, paparazzi images that are as shockingly real as your morning wake-up face.

So what happens when two people are willing to be transparent and authentic with one another? When the uncut and unfiltered version of you shows up, you naturally (without knowing) invite others to do the same thing – put down their guard and relax. Being yourself puts people at ease which begins to break the ice and make room for something worthwhile. I'm not suggesting that you skip brushing your teeth or wear slouchy cat pajamas but you get the point.

Building brands that people trust is no different. In fact, each of us is a brand unto ourselves with uniquely ownable characteristics. It's what others depend on us for and it's why they are able to make emotional connections with us. In conversations with clients we ask probing questions to dig up and identify what makes their product or service "better, different or special." As tedious as this practice can be, we are disciplined around this subject because we know that their success is dependent upon it. It's what we call their brand promise and what they can legitimately dominate with in the market, completely and honestly. It's a promise that says 'I will always be this way and that's what you can count on. Always.'

Generally speaking, I'm fairly casual. On a really good day, you might find me wearing full make up and an outfit that does not include jeans. But the real me is a somewhat casual, light-hearted blonde with a touch of mascara and lip gloss. I have a nerdy but sunny, laid back disposition and that's the person I really want you to know.

Embarrassing as this is to admit, in some of my earlier coffees, I would dress a little nicer and always wear full makeup to put my best face forward. But over time, I let go of those things because what really connected me to these one-of-kind individuals was a genuine conversation. It had nothing to do with the personification of my ideal self or how I was dressed. Nor did it matter if I could articulate my 10 second elevator pitch with eloquence and ease.

A coffee is a fairly short time period, usually about an hour. To make a connection and start something valuable you must, without fail, open up those steel curtains and take a chance that the person you're meeting will do the same with you.

Getting to know someone new takes practice. So practice being yourself, practice being open about who you are and what you care about. There is no better advice than the age-old adage of "be yourself."

THE REAL THEM

If you really want what's best for your future community, your goal should be to focus on the person sitting across from you. It's their experiences and unique qualities that make the relationship magic happen. And, it's how you will learn to add value for everyone involved.

If you have an open mind, it is rarely boring and there is always something valuable to be discovered – a new point of view, an idea that inspires you, a way to help and advise *them* or simply an enjoyable time with another human being.

Intrigued by my upcoming coffee #46, I was eager to meet the art professor. His daughter was someone I had met the prior month over dinner with a mutual friend. She had impressed me with her and her father's global initiative – to share his love of art with children in developing nations. The two of them would travel to hospitals with their art supplies to brighten the dreary walls and hearts of the local people. They would involve the children by laying out canvases and offering paints and brushes so they could explore art for the first time in their lives. I couldn't wait to meet him. I've always been interested in teaching a class on the importance of business in the field of art, and that was one of the programs he taught. A tenured and retired professor of art history at a notable local college, I thought our mutual interest in art would be the center of discussion. But what I didn't expect was the fascinating journey that our three-hour coffee would take me on.

The gentle professor was born in Argentina, the son of two immigrants from Europe. His family had enough wealth and position in Argentina that his life eventually became at risk when he witnessed his friends being kidnapped and ransomed during the country's Dirty War. In fear of their lives, he fled with his wife to the United States as a young adult. In a devastating blow, the professor lost his precious wife to cancer. By God's grace, he faithfully marched on to raise his five small children to be well-adjusted and happy adults.

With his children grown and out of the house, the professor had joined a small group of global historians whose mission was to find and preserve art that pre-dates the Renaissance and other well-documented art periods. On one of his expeditions, his team was searching for a legendary cave painting that was thought to have originated during the time of John the Baptist, a foremost figure in the bible known for baptizing Jesus himself. The supposed cave painting was said to depict Christian symbols and its legend was famous in the area, having been passed down through the generations. A Christian himself, the professor set out to confirm its existence.

As he approached the land where he believed it was located, he was greeted by an elderly man... and his gun. But, as he tells the story, the gun didn't scare him. With trepidation and knowing his intentions were pure, he bravely moved toward the loaded weapon – believing that God would guard him from harm. As he and the man came closer, he tried reasoning with him saying "Please, don't shoot me. I am only looking for information and I believe that something great is on your land." The man began to listen and just then, the professor noticed that his wife had some kind of arthritis or debilitating ailment. In a moment of desperation to make a small connection, he offered the man a bottle of Ibuprofen from his backpack. He said, "Give this to your wife to feel better." When he returned the next day, the man's demeanor had changed significantly toward him. He was welcoming and grateful to him for easing his wife's pain. In return for his kindness, he not only allowed him to explore, but took him to see a familiar cave on his land .

Just as the stories had been told, he found the legendary painting. It was one of the most incredible discoveries of his life and career.

Upon close examination of the painting's symbolism, it was clear that the artist's intent was to document what he learned about Christianity. The professor theorized that, given the estimated age of the painting, the artist had heard the gospel directly from John the Baptist himself. But, during that time, it was illegal to believe in Christianity so the painter had cautiously hidden his artwork away from persecuting eyes. Today it is a protected artifact.

That day, I learned that sometimes a really, real hour... or three, can lead to the greatest discoveries.

DARE TO BE REAL.

SOUL FILTER

"YOU GET WHAT YOU GIVE. SO GIVE GOOD STUFF."

So the road may be paved with good intentions but so are communities. And, the foundation is laid by you – a person of integrity who genuinely cares about the interests of others. Yes, the idea sounds like baking cookies for the world and on paper it reminds me of my sweet daughter who thanks God each night for unicorns. But, I realized around coffee #3 or so that my intentions needed to run through a soul filter of sorts. If we approach each new business meeting with an attitude of "What's in it for me?" we will launch ourselves into a backwards way of thinking. This thinking is dangerous because it limits the possibilities of being in community with someone.

45

It's cloaked as a version of conditional love except in the business context.

In contrast, unconditional love is most often used to describe the love between family members, comrades in arms and between those in highly committed relationships. This kind of love hinges on affection, friendship, eros, and charity.

In psychology, unconditional love refers to a state of mind in which one's goal is to increase the welfare of another, despite any evidence of selfish benefit. We need to remove the idea of mining for future business from the equation all together. Let's just run our souls through a purification filter before any new interaction. This will prepare us to be respectful, straightforward, trustworthy and above all, charitable.

As a parent, there are days when I have to gently remind my children that the world does not revolve around them. They want so desperately to be the most important living being in the house whose needs, above all others, matter most. And at times, their behavior reminds me of the spoiled and temperamental character, Veruca Salt, from Willy Wonka and The Chocolate Factory. Not a pretty picture.

So why, as adults, do we go into new business relationships with the same kind of approach? Why do we spend time calculating the outcome, pre-screening the candidate for potential gain and then strategizing our best sales pitch? Intentions, intentions and more intentions. I am the first to admit that I have been guilty on some level of doing all of these things either intentionally or unintentionally. It's human nature to want to be heard, feel important and have our desires met. But controlling these urges and having the right mindset in advance will create the right, open environment for making a genuine connection during your time with someone.

Be inspiring, be helpful, be a good listener but do not be self-absorbed. Understanding that it's not about you, will not only draw the person in closer but it will clear the table for new opportunities to be created. We've talked about why it's important to build community but this is *how* you do it. It's not a complex equation of strategy and posturing. It is simply sitting across the table from a stranger and looking for a way to make a positive impact on their business, life or day.

One of my favorite memories from 2012 was coffee #22 spent with a colleague's wife. She and I had never met but her husband had been our IT consultant for many years. She was a very seasoned designer working for an art museum in Uptown Charlotte, NC. It was easy getting to know her and swapping stories about the industry and work we had both been proud of throughout our similar careers. As we talked, she openly shared with me her overwhelming struggles in dealing with mismanagement and organizational chaos. We spent a good part of our discussion brainstorming ideas for managing and laughing at this ridiculousness. In fact, things had become so culturally depressed for her that she and her closest colleague had started a "Happy Journal" as a way to encourage one another each day. A brilliant and selfless idea.

Coming into our coffee with an unconditional outlook and purified soul, I offered the only thing I had available which was my ability to listen and empathize. Afterwards, I came back to my office to continue my day but couldn't help thinking about how much she was hurting. Many thoughts stayed with me from our coffee and I was satisfied having spent a genuine hour with her. As the day went on, I received the most sincere email and what felt like a gift to me, "Jenny, it was so good to have someone to talk with over lunch that understands what I'm going through. Today, you were my entry into the Happy Journal and I just wanted you to know that." To me, it doesn't get much better than that!

PEOPLE WANT TO DO BUSINESS
WITH PEOPLE THEY LIKE.
AND, PEOPLE WILL ONLY LIKE YOU
WHEN YOU HAVE THE RIGHT INTENTIONS.

HARVESTING THE BEANS

Have you ever wondered what might have happened to Marty McFly in 1985 if he had not traveled back in time to fix all that went wrong? I have. As a kid of the '80s I loved this movie, but now in my 40s I see how this teaches a valuable lesson. One, single encounter can set into motion a chain of events that will impact your future. I realize this is not earth shattering material but it does quickly illustrate something I've come to experience post-50 Coffees – *harvesting of the beans*. It's the return on your investment of time and energy and giving to your most valuable asset, your bean crop (community.) This return comes back to us in all shapes and sizes.

We don't expect it but it is a natural bi-product of living in authentic community with others.

In the early fall of 2011, the year before my caffeinated awakening, I had one coffee with a lovely and savvy women who worked in my industry. My coffee with her would become the first seed to be firmly planted into the rich soil of my community garden.

We had an easy conversation getting to know each other and when the topic turned to developing new business, her area of expertise, she generously offered some useful insights. A seasoned sales woman for one of the nation's largest printers, she is uniquely gifted with the ability to open any door. I was fascinated and in awe of her strengths in bringing in new accounts. In fact, I seriously considered offering her a sales role in our firm on the spot. When I joked about the idea, she graciously declined. But the point is, she *was* the epitome of a well-intentioned, unconditional first coffee and I knew we would continue to nurture that relationship. She was setting an example for me long before my 50 Coffees adventure. And, it was ultimately my coffee with her that would turn out to make a tremendous impact on the success of my business.

Almost an entire year after that first coffee with my new sales dynamo friend, I received an interesting call that went something like this, "Hi, Sales Dynamo friend mentioned that you do work for major financial institutions in the southeast. I wonder if we could get together to talk about an idea for one of my clients." So, I did the obvious thing and said, "I would love to meet with you and learn more. Let's have coffee." And coffee #20 was on the schedule.

A few conversations and proposals later with coffee #20 and we would secure the second largest account in our firm's history – all thanks to my coffee from 2011 with Sales Dynamo. This new account has earned a considerable amount of revenue over the past several years and has opened the door to new projects – adding fuel to our creative engines.

There have been other, similar success stories like this one and they all point back to the same theme of relationships + reach = return. When you build new relationships you expand your reach. And when you have a broader and deeper community of trusted colleagues to collaborate with, the return comes in the form of revenue, resources and reward.

Beyond the obvious financial benefits that come from expanding our reach into the business community, we have experienced other benefits that are equally bountiful. In the chapter on "business survival" I talked about how our firm is structured as a virtual team of people and that we rely on their talents for a wide range of initiatives. Being in relationship with a broader community of people has given us a deeper pool of talent to work with.

I've worked with several of my coffees from 2012 but specifically, the timing of coffee #7 was perfect. We had been working with a client on some mid-level marketing initiatives. They were a good fit for us but not the meaty, strategic projects we enjoy sinking our teeth into. Several months after #7, one of our clients asked us to develop a "business pitch" for their CEO. They wanted it animated in Power-Point because that's what the CEO was most comfortable using. We had developed other pitches in the past with strategic messaging and creative but PowerPoint was not 100% in our wheelhouse. That's where #7 comes in. I had learned in our coffee that he is passionate about developing pitches and in fact, he had been involved in several for a well-known think-tank organization in Charlotte. Not only was I excited at the idea of having him on my team, influencing the outcome with his genuine passion for pitches but he also enjoyed PowerPoint. Homerun! Had we not met, we may have sidelined the project as not being the right fit for our firm.

Since then, Moving Ideas has enjoyed many fruits of seeds planted in first coffees. Coffee #23, turned friend, has been instrumental in helping me write this book. I've come to love her sense of humor and respect her marketing savvy. She gifted me with one of the funniest, most memorable lines from any of my coffees. Waiting at the counter for her arrival and not knowing what to expect, in walks a very stylish woman who was obviously looking for someone. Over the ambient noises of the coffee shop, we introduced ourselves and in her cool Australian accent, she boldly said, "Is this some kind of blind dating for friends?" I knew we would get along just fine and over the past few years, we've spent valuable time working together and inspiring one another's goals.

I've lived and witnessed first-hand what awesome outcomes there are when two people come together for coffee. People are fascinating and I've yet to meet one person that was like another.

My son joined our local pack of Cub Scouts as a Tiger last fall. He proudly wears their traditional blue Class A uniform with all of the beginner emblems for entry into the Boy Scouts of America community. It's pretty plain right now but I know that, over time, he'll earn more of the unique and intricately embroidered patches that come from investing in the organization. When you look at them closely, each is beautiful in its own way. Each has a significant meaning and its own story to tell.

The people we meet are the same way. We earn their trust and their stories become a part of our story.

THE IMMEDIATE AND LONG-TERM IMPACTS OF
MEETING JUST ONE PERSON CANNOT BE MEASURED.
THERE ARE SIMPLY NO LIMITS TO THE IMPACT THAT
ONE PERSON CAN MAKE ON ANOTHER.

YOUR 50

So what do all cities, large or small, have in common? Human population. Charlotte is the 15th largest city in the country, attracting more than 500 newcomers each week. If you look at the number of LinkedIn connections you have and compare them to the number of people living in your city or town, I promise you... you'll have plenty of coffees to schedule.

Having a catch-up coffee with #19 , an investment broker, it occurred to me that you can never make too many introductions or have too many coffees. As he and I sat discussing some recent challenges, I immediately thought of a long-time friend in the insurance business whose offering could be complementary. Again, I did the natural thing and sent a group email suggesting they meet. But, my great epiphany that morning was the shear depth and number of opportunities there are to expand our reach. My colleagues had both lived and worked in the Charlotte region for many years, in closely related industries, but had never met. Huh! You think you live in a small town and then, snap! You don't!

That being said, you could have multiple coffees with the same individual and continue to deepen that one relationship over time. With the right attitude of wanting to add value, you are continuously learning more about them as their business is evolving. And in most cases, the same holds true for them. They will continue to learn more about you, your business and where it can add value in the community. This ongoing social approach is a kind of "business soul food," there's always enough of it to go around as long as you're willing to generously give it out.

So let's start your own 50 Coffees!

FIRST, ESTABLISH A CRITERIA

Who do you want to get to know? Or rather, what do you want your future community to look like? Will it include a wide and diverse range of professionals or do you prefer to surround yourself with folks from your industry? I suggest keeping your criteria simple and straightforward and you'll be able to determine which coffees make the most sense.

Mine can be summed up as *any respectable professional in my local business community who is referred by a colleague or friend.* Aligning with my value system, it made more sense to make connections with those who were already held in high regard by those I respected. I decided early on that I was open to individuals both in and outside of my field. You can establish any criteria you like but remember, the more restrictions you place on your future community, the less opportunity you have at a deeply rich group of people to share it with.

What not to do.... It's critical not to confuse your sales lead criteria with your community criteria. Most people you have coffee with will never buy from you directly but they will remember you when the opportunity is right to recommend you to someone else.

SCHEDULE YOUR FIRST COFFEE

There are numerous people that float in and out of your world that you've probably never given more than five minutes to. I was the queen of acquaintances and sometimes oblivious to the working lives and passions of the people around me. Being intentional with my 50 Coffees has turned the microcosm of my business pond into a coral reef rich enough to sustain abundant life and business growth.

Make a list of a few people you've known for some time. Then, ask yourself, "If I had to recommend this person to a colleague, would I have something meaningful to say about them" and more importantly, ask yourself, "If they had to recommend me, what would they say?" If the answer is that you don't know them well enough to answer, then you've got the right list. So finding the right first coffee does not require a process chart or board meeting – only that they fit your community criteria.

Now that you've got your list, contact them and get your first coffee on the calendar. You can reach out directly or ask a trusted colleague to make the introduction for you. Be open and honest about why you would like to meet for coffee – which is to get to know more people in your business community.

Here are a couple of introductory scenarios and emails for initiating a first coffee:

Scenario No. 1: Your colleague/friend Maria V. recommended that you meet her contact, Phillip B.

Subject Line: Maria V. recommended you

Hi Phillip,

Maria V. and I are colleagues from (insert how you are affiliated) and she recommended that I reach out to you. I was sharing with her my goal to get to know more like-minded people in the business community. She thought of you and, because I value her opinion, I wondered if you would like to have coffee in the next week or so. I'm happy to meet somewhere that is convenient for you!

All my best,
Jenny

Note: Be sure to cc: Maria on your email so that Phillip will have more confidence in the introduction.

———

Scenario No. 2: John D. is someone you've met before but would like to get to know further.

Subject Line: Coffee to catch up?

Hi John,

I'm not sure if you remember meeting at the Gala Event in Charlotte last spring but we had a nice conversation about (insert specifics here). I believe strongly in building relationships with people I respect in the business community but it's difficult to really get to know people at those kinds of events. Would you have time to meet for coffee in the next week or so? I would genuinely enjoy learning more about what you do.

All my best,
Jenny

Note: Personalizing this message with details of how you met will help you to rebuild a connection even if it has been a long time since your original meeting.

NOW GO MEET 49 MORE

The best way to meet coffee number two is to ask coffee number one who they think you should meet next. I aimlessly fumbled my way into my first dozen coffee meetings. Until it occurred to me that you have to ask.

"I am trying to build community. Is there anyone that you know who might benefit from meeting me?"

"Is there anyone you think I should get to know?"

Most people genuinely want to help you connect with people they know and if you can, try to reciprocate the courtesy. Don't worry, if your community is still small, there will be plenty of opportunities later.

COFFEE TIPS

Don't cancel. Reschedule only under rare circumstances.

When you cancel, you're burning an already flimsy bridge and communicating "I'm only interested in getting to know you when it's 100% convenient for me." That's not a good way to start any relationship.

Do a little homework.

LinkedIn and other social media sources are a good way to learn about who you're going to meet ahead of time. It also makes recognizing that person in a crowded coffee house much easier.

Coffee isn't mandatory.

The idea of building community is about spending time with someone, face-to-face, in order to get to know them better. Whether this happens in a coffee house, restaurant or over a bucket of balls at the driving range, the event is merely a technicality. Coffees are easier and less expensive but not the only way. Stay open to the other person's comfort level and be accommodating.

Stay organized.

Learning and remembering names is something I have to work hard at myself. When you set a goal to meet 50 people in a year, on the recommendation of others, you can quickly lose track of *how* you met *who*. But it's important to keep track of those details. And, I agree with Albert Einstein's concept of never committing anything to memory that you don't have to. Here is a journaling tool I developed that helped me reach my goal. I hope it's helpful for you.

50 Coffees Journal

Cup	Coffee	Date	Barista	E/T/C
1.	Who you met	When	How you met	Email Text Call
2.				
3.				
4.				
5.				
6.				
7.				
8.				
9.				
10.				

You can download a pdf of this worksheet at my50coffees.com.

COFFEE CUPS

———~~~———

While researching and writing this book, there were several people and their stories that made a lasting impression on my journey through 50 Coffees. Here are just a few that I hope will inspire you to build your community and ultimately change the course of your business and life.

COFFEE #1

You may be wondering, who was my first coffee? Well, as luck would have it, he called me. I came into my office with the voice mail button blinking. Listening to his message I distinctly remember a joyful feeling of confirmation come over me. #1 was a colleague of a colleague who wanted to meet for coffee and learn more about Moving Ideas. Did he also have a coffee goal? Did my new plan just kick *itself* off without me lifting a finger? I think so! My eyes and ears were at full attention during this inaugural coffee and I learned a few key things that would carry me through to 50:

1. You have to put yourself out there. Make the call and ask someone to have coffee.
2. Don't be afraid to be honest with others about your desire to meet new people.
3. You're not the only one who wants to meet for coffee.

COFFEE #8

Have you ever been in the same room with a dark roast personality who is so bold and smooth that they literally hold the entire group hostage with their presence? Meet coffee #8. Some might be put off by their unapologetic confidence but I found him refreshing during a book review presentation. It was an intimate gathering of entrepreneurs, most of which I didn't know. We sat around a conference room table discussing insights from a well-known best seller. Unlike me, he bravely shared and challenged relevant points made by everyone in the room. We shook hands afterward and I suggested we schedule a coffee – something I would not have initiated pre-50 Coffees. A believer in community himself, he gladly made time to meet. He introduced me to respected colleagues and is an all-around rock star of a person. Having experienced being in community with him and others, I have found that each person has something valuable to contribute. When you generously give of yourself everyone wins. Dark roast has been a good friend over the years and I'm grateful to be in community with him. Particularly, he deserves kudos for bringing me through one of my more memorable business moments. Our firm had the opportunity to give a pitch to a group of suppliers from a very large, global auto manufacturer. Whether I liked it or not it was go-time for me to step up, be a leader for my team and make the pitch. I'm not a public speaker... AT ALL... never and next to death, speaking in public is a huge fear of mine. In a room full of people where the spot light is on me, whatever words I plan to say are somehow highjacked by my throat muscles and it's over before it begins. But... we had a few weeks to prepare and I would need every spare minute to concept, write and practice. This really needed to be good and I hoped to challenge myself past my comfort zone. Dark roast was a huge help. He jumped in, listened to my ideas, offered crucial suggestions and then coached my delivery. I sincerely couldn't have done it as well without him. On pitch day, my heart raced furiously and I thought my legs would not carry me up to that podium. But they did and I was a little stronger for having been so prepared. As it turns out, it was an above-average speech according to my colleagues in the audience. That introduction, plus our time meeting with suppliers at the event, earned us a place on their corporate supplier list.

COFFEE #48

You never know what kind of day someone is having. She walked into the coffee shop with an expression that reads "I think I'm going to be sick." I'm not even sure why she didn't cancel. I would have. On the heels of a bad day, the last thing I feel like doing is meeting someone new and chatting for an hour. But she did anyway, which is something I admire about her. She filled me in on what her day had entailed and how the months leading up to that day were career torture. Having worked within a company whose values were not aligned with hers and feeling trapped by no other job prospects, she stepped out on a very unsteady limb and quit. Not knowing what the future held, she had reached her limit. I tried to be a shoulder to lean on. Sometimes that's all you can do. Often it's all someone needs to flip a bad day into a better one. Over the next couple of weeks, I happily pushed every new job opportunity that came across my desk her way. She needed help and I leaned on my community for support. What kind of community would it be if we did not try to help? It wasn't long until she landed somewhere terrific.

COFFEE #2

Coffees don't always have to be with people you've never met. It's a good idea to learn more about acquaintances who have buzzed in and out of your work life, especially those who live in your immediate community. That's how #2 happened. Moving Ideas had been searching for a creative director and he was one of the candidates we interviewed. We couldn't afford him at the time but he was a talented designer and, now several years later, I wondered what he was up to. When we reconnected for coffee he surprised me. Designing only part-time, he had made a dramatic career move into business coaching. He had always been passionate about helping people with personal growth and had turned his passion into a professional pursuit. Meeting him again was perfect timing for our firm. Having struggled to

69

grow, we had never spent much time on our business planning and goals. He suggested a half day coaching session which eventually turned into a much longer engagement. My business partner, Yvette Salerno, and I stretched and changed in ways we could not have anticipated. It truly made a positive impact on us personally and on our company. Specifically, we had struggled with our natural roles as owners in the firm. My role was generally creative and hers was more account-facing and operational. In an unspoken way, a friendly tug of war would break out between us when a client presented a new idea to us. While I was easily excited by the endless possibilities, Yvette would be asking the hard questions about viability and budget, bringing reality into the discussion. In one of our sessions with #2, she confessed that this made her feel like a kill-joy and he offered a brilliant solution. He suggested fresh new titles that would highlight our strengths, "Chief Possibilities Officer" for me and "Chief Reality Officer" for her. By intentionally and playfully acknowledging our unique roles, we brought a balanced approach to our clients – one that was both creative and sensible. This new dynamic has enhanced our appreciation for one another and become something we rely on daily. As you might imagine, coach is now having a record year and help-ing others break through.

COFFEE #32

If humans could be superheroes, she would have a cape of her own. Her super power would be the abil-ity to build up others so that they can achieve their full potential in life. Not to mention that she is also a keynote speaker, Ph.D., business owner, executive leadership coach and, in her spare time, a very tal-ented artist. What an honor it was to spend time with her that day, just as it has been to get to know her over the last several years. Meeting at a busy Pan-era Bread in Charlotte, she first greeted me with a genuine smile and enthusiasm. She had heard about my goal and wanted to know more about 50 "cups," as she called it. Building community was not a new concept for her and she quickly launched our con-versation into a brainstorm of ways that we might be able to collaborate and work together. Do you remember the pitch I talked about earlier? The one I so nervously gave to a large automotive manufac-turer? Yes, that opportunity was a direct result of our first coffee. She personally invited us to participate at her client's vendor supplier expo and you know the rest of story. As a strong advocate for diversity and inclusion in the workplace, she partners closely with corporate human resource divisions to build teams, grow leaders and shape the pathways for women and minorities to advance. Superhero-ish don't you think?

COFFEE #18

You're not going to hit it off with everyone you meet. And that's ok! Keep having coffees and building your community with people you like.

COFFEE #25

Mac's Speed Shop in Charlotte is home to some of the best BBQ you can find this side of the Mississippi. They probably do serve coffee but #25 and I had pulled pork that day instead. Her husband and I had belonged to a young entrepreneurs organization and cut our business teeth together years prior. Catching up one day I mentioned my coffee goal and he suggested meeting his lovely and brilliant wife. We spent a few minutes swapping "what I do's" and I learned about her role as a top executive for a large financial advisory. But then we launched into topics that were a lot more fun like Panther's football, our kids and shoes. Such a joyful and dynamic person with a real energy for life. You can find her running half marathons, hiking mountains, traveling abroad and doing whatever she puts her mind to. I keep telling her that "when I grow up I want to be just like you." If you are committed to growing your community, I promise that you will meet many fantastic individuals along the way, just as I have.

COFFEE #28

Thanks in large part to coffee #28, you're able to read this text in a printed or digital form. After self-publishing his own engaging book, "Pod Castaway," in 2016 he graciously offered to take me through the process and help me across this finish line. Given his expertise in content strategy and social media communications, we have spent several hours over coffee swapping questions, ideas and opinions on a wide range of topics. He's a straight shooter, a no BS kind of person with a huge heart and ethical at the core. When he heard what I was doing, he shared his biggest pet peeve about coffee meetings. He believes and I agree, that if you're going to invite someone to have coffee to only "pick their brain" and basically use the time as a gold mining session, the least you can do is buy. I'm sure he doesn't really care about the $4.50 expense. It's just the principle of the thing.

So, takers need not apply here! And 50 Coffees is the furthest idea from having an agenda to pull useful information from generous people. I'm not telling you to cautiously share valuable insight because you should. I encourage everyone to give, give, give. Just be sure to run your intentions through the soul filter before a meeting. A special thank you to this guy, for being generous and real.

COFFEE #29

We're all just people in community with other people. My daughter's bus stop was full of parents each morning who gave a friendly smile and "hello." We might exchange a polite remark or two but as soon as the wheels went 'round, we drove off in separate directions. By the fall of my coffee year, I was more than half way to my goal of 50. I could not ignore the fact that my view of these typical, fast-paced situations had noticeably changed. These situations looked more like missed opportunities to genuinely connect with others. Without knowing, I had been glancing past the faces and stories and lives right in front of me, day in and day out – our neighbors, church members and other parents. It's common to sideline extra things when life is hectic and action packed. But now, I wanted to do something different and start having coffees with these familiar faces! I knew from other quick conversations that my soon-to-be #29 appreciated a good latte as much as I did and our kids regularly hung out together. So on the morning of our coffee I steamed lattes-for-two and toted them in a carafe down to her house. Conversation was effortless and we made a real and meaningful connection that went further than the busy chitchat. At the time, she was bravely battling cancer with the most remarkable and strong spirit. Sadly, last November, my beautiful friend gained her angel wings which left a very large hole in our community. She was known by so many for her warm and generous hugs which always had a way of making you feel unconditionally loved. For so many reasons, I count my blessings for choosing to spend time with her over and above the hectic pace of life. I may have started my coffee goal with growing my business in mind, but what I discovered was the community all around me in a richer, more significant way. Because we're just people in community with other people.

To Chip, my "dear old dad,"
it's finally done and
i hope you're smiling down
on me from Heaven.

98962414R00046

Made in the USA
Middletown, DE
10 November 2018